DON'T LET THE *UTIs* GRIND YOU DOWN

A true-life experience of avoiding URINARY TRACT INFECTIONS

Beverly Thompson

authorHOUSE®

AuthorHouse™ UK
1663 Liberty Drive
Bloomington, IN 47403 USA
www.authorhouse.co.uk
Phone: UK TFN: 0800 0148641 (Toll Free inside the UK)
     UK Local: 02036 956322 (+44 20 3695
     6322 from outside the UK)

Published by AuthorHouse   08/21/2020

ISBN: 978-1-7283-5451-4 (sc)
ISBN: 978-1-7283-5450-7 (e)

Print information available on the last page.

This book is printed on acid-free paper.

CONTENTS

ABOUT THE BOOK

Many women continue to suffer the distress caused by repeated UTIs without really knowing why. In this book I explain in some detail how I've managed to avoid these bacterial attacks which have plagued my life for about 40 years.

In sharing my ideas with other women who suffer with these infections, I hope to reduce the number of sufferers and point out the potential risks we are taking.

PREFACE

Some people go all through their lives without knowing what a UTI is. It is not a disease. It is not at all contagious. It is not a sexually transmitted infection. A *Urinary Tract Infection* can be a very painful but is usually a self-inflicted simple condition caused by bacteria in the wrong place. In this book I aim to explain the causes of the two most common water infections and how we can try to prevent them.

During this recollection of my past struggle with urine infections, I shall intimately share how I've managed to avoid a return of the UTI. The impact of UTIs throughout my own life has been disruptive and stressful, however one simple lifestyle change has made such a difference. I believe sharing my discovery with other women in this book will have a huge positive impact for women suffering infections worldwide. It should mean fewer calls to your doctor and fewer antibiotics in our lives. Prevention of any woman suffering a UTI must be worth talking about. Please compare my ideas with how your own lifestyle could cause recurring infections, then consider which changes you need to make in your everyday life.

Antibiotics are one cure for one UTI at a time, but in regular use they can also have detrimental side-effects and can be damaging to other organs. By explaining how to avoid the need for taking medications I hope we will all live healthier lives. Through perseverance I've now learned how to prevent further attacks and I feel confident that by making small adjustments to my daily routine I will remain UTI-free into the future (if I remember the golden rules).

In today's digital world there is so much advice online which claims to help UTI sufferers. Lots of opinions are available to read about on every search engine, but it's usually very basic guidelines or about research or patient backgrounds with very limited advice about treatment rather than prevention. Further into this article I have tips and hints about how to avoid risking irritation, as the intimate female body parts really don't need 'soap', just gentle cleansing.

You may be wondering why my personal experience should make a difference to your life, when we are all different. I'm just an ordinary woman in my fifties, and there are too many things left to enjoy in my life without suffering with UTIs. There are women all over the world who want to know how a UTI can be prevented, and by telling my own story with my own revelation, I would like to think I have helped other people. Medical information is freely available online for anyone who needs it, but can you find the information that will help you? I couldn't. During my own search for online help I was deeply disappointed with the results, as I was still having recurring infections that I needed to put an end to. I concentrated all of my efforts to seek the right information over the years, however not once have I seen any online advice relating to the lifestyle change I've made. So far this change has been 100% improvement in my life, and if it works for me it might just work for you.

In reading about my experiences it must be recognised that:

- The causes of my UTIs have not derived from serious illness or cancer treatments.
- This is a true life, very personal experience of a battle over recurrent UTIs
- I do not use any medical aids that could induce a UTI, such as a catheter.
- I do not claim to be an expert, only a woman who wants to help others to help themselves.
- Chemotherapy or immunosuppressive treatments will make you more vulnerable to infections.
- I am not a nurse or a GP and at no point in the whole of this article do I offer any complete cure.
- My experiences may not resolve UTIs caused by any other means than mentioned below and therefore may not be the answer you are looking for. Always consult your doctor for help

INTRODUCTION

Bacteria is everywhere; our skin is covered in it.

We cannot live without it, so to avoid
infection we must avoid the spread.

Each time a woman has a UTI, her chances of having recurrent infections will increase, and severe infections can lead to urosepsis, which can be fatal.

I am Beverly Thompson, a happily married working mum, now in my fifties. I've grown up battling with water infections and have succumbed to the fact that I am one of the minority of women who suffer regular UTIs. Some women do, some don't. It is all to do with the spread of 'bad' bacteria and I expect some women are built to deal with it better. During my working life I've come to realise there are lots of ordinary women, young and old who are suffering recurring 'water infections', and many needlessly so. My aim in writing this book is to condense vital information and my real-life experience all into one little book, with the aim of helping women to take better control of their bodies.

<u>Bodily functions:</u>

Urine under normal conditions has no bacteria in it. It is one of the body's waste products which is produced in the kidneys and travels down the ureters into the bladder. The bladder stores the urine until it is emptied by urinating through the urethra, (the tube connecting the bladder to the skin). A urinary tract infection (UTI) is usually the result of bacteria invading the urethra and travelling into the bladder, thus causing inflammation. Most UTIs are not serious, just very uncomfortable. In young girls water infections can disappear as fast as they arrived. By drinking plenty of water and taking paracetamol, their symptoms should improve. Sometimes it helps to have a hot water bottle handy to rest on the abdomen or between the thighs. However, many mature women will experience repeated infections as they get older and these can develop into a kidney infection if left untreated. Read about the connection between the ageing process and why UTI infections are on the increase in this article.

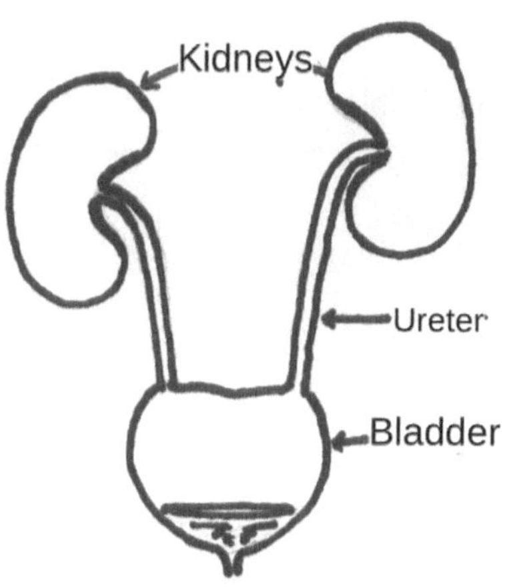

The function of the kidneys includes balancing your body's Ph level, and the production of hormones as well as potassium and sodium. Urine is the filtered liquid waste that's produced in these processes. Our kidneys are vitally important to our health, so if a UTI is left untreated in the bladder, the bacteria can then travel up to the kidneys. From there a bacterial infection of the kidneys creates cramping sensations which increase and eventually become unbearable. These cramps are known as renal colic. For me, renal colic starts within the first 24 hours of any water infection, due to having had years of recurrent infections. The onset is quite rapid and quickly develops into unbearable pain. I've been known to curl up on the waiting room floor in the GP surgery in agony whilst waiting for the doctor. The only effective treatment for me at this point is with antibiotics and dispersible co-codamol.

Worth knowing, is that if bacteria reaches the kidneys, it can create life threatening infection once it reaches the bloodstream. Avoid taking NSAIDs (non-steroidal anti-inflammatory drugs) like ibuprofen or aspirin if you think you may have a kidney infection as it's possible this could increase the risk of kidney problems. Always consult with your doctor about changes you make to any of your medications.

I have listed risks of infection under 6 different chapters:
The Basics
The Ageing Process
Knowing Cystitis
Personal Hygiene
Sexually Active Women
Staying Healthy

1

THE BASICS

It is a fact that around 10 out of 25 women suffer UTIs in their lifetime, as opposed to 3 out of 25 men. Some women have never had one. The difference in numbers between women and men is basically due to three facts:

1. The urinary tract in women is shorter than in men.
2. In a woman's body the urethra opening is closer to other bacterial sources than in men.
3. Young girls and older women have lower levels of the hormone estrogen in their bodies. This makes them more vulnerable to infection around the genitals as bacteria will flourish where there is less hormonal activity.

The female body is unfortunately very susceptible to bacteria easily spreading between the openings which are very close to each other. During a lifetime 40% of all women will experience UTIs. Female genitalia has 3 openings (excluding the clitoris). We have the urinary tract for expelling urine at the front, then the vagina for intercourse/birthing and finally the rectum for faecal waste. Although the urinary tract is the smallest opening, it is also the most vulnerable. The vagina and the rectum are quite close and these both have large numbers of natural bacteria which should not be transferred to the urethra. Our bodies are usually moist in this area and moisture is the perfect carrier of unwanted bacteria. Many people go through life with little more than a bit of discomfort from the odd water infection and they think nothing of it, whilst others can be traumatised, with pain and constant visits to the bathroom. This can all be avoided with extra daily care.

Recognising a UTI

With infection comes a whole variety of unpleasant symptoms. These include a burning sensation when you try to pass urine, passing less urine than you feel you need to, frequency of the urge to pee (which never really goes away even after several minutes waiting on the toilet), fatigue, headaches and sometimes nausea. You may also find that your urine smells unusually bad and is cloudy. If you have had an infection before and think you can cure these symptoms by simply drinking water or by taking herbal remedies or analgesia - you are mistaken, it's now too late. Bacteria have already taken hold, causing inflammation inside your bladder. You must call your GP for advice.

A valid point at this stage is that carers of elderly people who require toilet assistance may have noted strong dark or even smelly urine in their patients. Please do not be alarmed at first as this could be normal for them, or they could be dehydrated, so always get a urine test done with their GP just in case.

Prevention of any kind of infection is of course far better than a week of antibiotics from your GP, as many of these have unpleasant side-effects. Repeat doses of antibiotics are not good for other vital organs in the long term either. So, if you're ready to assess your way of life and the impact this has on your wellbeing, read on...

THE AGEING PROCESS

As we all age, it's a fact that the bladder muscles become weaker. Both men and women suffer this fate which will result in more frequent trips to the toilet. The bladder is made to expand when it becomes laden with urine and muscles contract in order to empty it. This is not always as straightforward as it sounds. Because the muscles around the bladder become weaker and the opening can become restricted as we all age, not all of the urine is expelled each time and we tend to get what's called urinary retention.

Around the age of 40, urinary retention affected my life and resulted in several water infections every year. It became a vicious cycle and I had some investigations done at hospital. On further examination, the neck of my bladder had become thickened with age, which meant that I was unable to completely empty it on each visit to the toilet. This caused a small amount of urine becoming stagnant in my bladder for long periods, over and over, eventually creating an infection. I was told this is quite a common problem as people do not fully empty their bladder often enough. It happens to men around the same age too, who may suffer an enlarged prostate gland. Since writing this article I know of another woman 10 years younger than me who has recently had the same experience.

A small operation as an in-patient at hospital for one night can 'widen' the neck of the bladder in order to empty it all every time. This remedy has some pitfalls however, as until you can train the bladder to close by working the right muscles regularly, there can be slight unexpected leakage when you cough, sneeze, laugh or run. Nowadays I can empty my bladder as normal. I always wait a few seconds after I've finished, then consciously try to push more urine out. Sure enough there is always a bit more to come. Honestly, it's worth double checking it's completely empty each time. Be forewarned, that even a year after this operation, my haste to exit a bathroom once resulted in embarrassing leakage I was not prepared for!

I do appreciate that many of you will already know about this kind of leakage even without infections, as we now reach so-called 'middle age', and there are many protective and discreet products on the market that will help us to cope. However, we all should continue to work the bladder 'sphincter' muscle to keep it working effectively and try to prevent any form of incontinence from weak muscles. Make yourself a promise not to let a leaky bladder spoil your future!

There is an exercise that can be done discreetly at any time if you stand, sit or lie down. To do this, just imagine you are squeezing a pencil held inside your vagina as tight as you can, and aim to hold it for 5 seconds... "count one and two and three and four and five" in steady rhythm.

Feel the squeeze? Once you have practiced this for a few weeks you can also do this once or twice on each visit to the toilet. You must be patient as this technique takes time to work, but within a few weeks you should be able to interrupt the constant flow of urine, giving you better control. By consciously doing the vaginal squeeze you are subconsciously using the bladder muscles at the urethra as well. Just tense the muscles around the vagina for a few seconds, and repeat 5 times. Don't forget to breathe normally whilst doing this as it's tempting to take a breath and hold it, which may be uncomfortable and could make you feel dizzy.

By practicing this exercise you will improve your bladder control. Whether you're standing in a shopping queue, driving your car, working at your desk or just watching tv, you can make a world of difference to you waterworks and your potential sex life. I often perform the 'imaginary pencil squeeze' for up to 10 seconds whilst I'm driving to work. Nobody knows. This advantage over the urinary flow may even come in handy when your visit to a toilet may be rudely interrupted by a partner and you need to suddenly stop - perhaps to take part in a conversation. Once you are able to pause the urine flow with better muscle control you should no longer have leakage accidents. There will also be times as we all get older that you will be grateful you can choose not to pass water. Just to add, for your first few attempts at this whilst on the toilet or following a UTI infection, the squeeze of the muscles can sometimes create a stinging effect in the urethra. On these occasions don't hold the urine back, release it all and try again after some recovery time.

Worth noting, there are other medical reasons why your kidneys can become painful and infected such as kidney stones, and these should be referred to a GP. My own experience has not been influenced by any of those other conditions.

3

KNOWING CYSTITIS

You may be wondering about the difference between cystitis and a UTI. These are actually both inflammation which can be caused by bacteria, yeast, acidic foods and drink or allergies to products.

In medical terms an *'itis'* is an inflammation and cystitis means inflammation of the bladder. It is usually caused by bacteria from the body called E.coli getting into the urethra causing irritation and inflammation. It can be a painful and unsettling condition, causing frequent trips to the toilet. The irritation can cause pain in your lower abdomen pelvic area and even lower back, and will usually make you feel like urinating more often. A burning pain when urinating is the most common symptom. You may even feel a strong urge or need to urinate but only get a few drops. This is because the bladder is so irritated that it makes you feel like you have to urinate, even when you don't have much urine in your bladder. At times, you may lose control and leak urine. Attempting to pass more urine creates a stinging or burning sensation which lingers for long after your efforts fail. Then, having resigned yourself to pain and failure you leave the bathroom only to feel the instant need to go again. There are products available as a powder to dissolve in water, or as a drink, which you can purchase over-the-counter at the local pharmacy. These can offer some relief in the early stages by counteracting the contents inside your bladder hence reducing inflammation. Drinking plenty of water is also important to help to flush it out of your body, but this does not offer instant physical relief.

Symptoms often include pelvic pain
and the urge to pee frequently

Urgency to pee with a limited flow
and a burning sensation.

Prevention

Cranberry juice has been used as a natural treatment for preventing bladder infections for generations. According to a 2012 review, cranberry juice and cranberry tablets show some promise as a remedy for women who frequently get bladder irritation. It's all due to something called D-Mannose which is a simple sugar frequently used to help prevent and treat mild UTIs. It is available naturally in cranberries, (if you've never tried them, they are quite bitter). This D-Mannose creates a coating on the lining of the bladder, therefore preventing bacteria from attaching to it. Just try real cranberry juice in a glass, (not a juice drink or a mixture, but fresh unsweetened cranberry juice) and you will notice when the glass is empty it leaves a thin film on the inside. Think of this as an example of how it can prevent bacteria from living inside the bladder. Bear in mind that D-mannose is a type of natural sugar and may not be suitable for anyone with sugar related conditions such as diabetes. Real cranberry juice (not substitute or cranberry drink) does help these symptoms, however cystitis in any form needs medical attention and your GP should have the best advice. There are popular beliefs in natural 'berry' products listed online, however you must be aware that prolonged ingestion of these so-called treatments can cause kidney and liver damage too, as can anti-inflammatory medicines and antibiotics. Powders bought over-the-counter and dissolved in water do give some relief, but try not to rely on medication that can cause other problems further down the line.

I have suffered since childhood with urinary tract infections without knowing why. Only now I can see how it has been partly due to my age, but mostly due to my lifestyle. Cystitis was a regular occurrence for me when I was a little girl in the 1960's. My mother became very worried and we had regular visits to the doctor's surgery. I had some tests at hospital to make sure that my kidneys were working properly. I remember being injected with a blue dye that would show up on an x-ray so they could see how well my kidneys worked. This was quite traumatic at only 6 years old, having a huge machine over my abdomen taking pictures. The results were never explained to me, but I do know that my kidneys are my weak point and have been susceptible to infection and maybe even kidney stones at some point, but these have never been found. I also underwent a cystoscopy to check for any causes inside my bladder, but the lining was normal.

Potential causes:

As I grew older I learned of the connection between 'attacks' of cystitis and the use of certain types of soap, especially some of the very perfumed ones and some bubble bath products. Moving into adulthood I was aware that if I bathed, it had to be just plain water, and I was careful with soap. I began to recognise which sanitary products or feminine wipes caused me an irritation. Perfumed products such as creams, washing products, fabric softeners, beauty products and feminine sprays can all be irritants for the urethra. I avoid new perfumed products whenever possible, just using coal tar soap which I prefer, and certain washing powders that I have learned to trust over time. When I was in my 40's I asked my GP if there were foods that could cause this pain. He suggested that I avoid tomatoes, knowing that my kidneys could be affected by small kidney stones which dissolved eventually. So, I now restrict my tomato consumption (which thankfully I don't miss).

In contrast to 'bacteria', I can guarantee to get attacks of cystitis when I drink certain things. It's as though the acid in certain drinks affects the Ph balance in my bladder, and I know that I am going to suffer with cystitis the following day. The drinks I personally have to avoid are cider, lager, prosecco and white wine. The affect of these drinks is not instantaneous, they seem to affect me if I have more than just one small glass. So, at Christmastime, I treat myself with a small glass of prosecco diluted with 50% orange juice, like a Buck's Fizz, which means I'm less likely to get discomfort. When I just fancy a refreshing lager drink I will always add a few drops of blackcurrant cordial or lemonade and just have one half pint glass, that's all. Red wine and drinks made from acidic fruits can also upset the contents of the bladder. A favourite health drink of mine is a quarter of fresh lemon squeezed into a cup with boiling water over it, leaving the lemon in the cup. It is recommended for detoxifying the system especially first thing in the morning, however, having regular acidic drinks will raise the risk of inflammation inside the bladder. If any of you can relate to this, just restrict the amount of acidic drinks if possible.

Based on medical research, certain foods and drinks can cause irritation in your bladder, including:

- Coffee, tea and carbonated drinks, even without caffeine.
- Alcohol.
- Certain acidic fruits — oranges, grapefruits, lemons and limes — and fruit juices.
- Spicy foods.
- Tomato-based products.
- Chocolate.

4

PERSONAL HYGIENE

Using a toilet is easy....or is it? You are unlikely to catch infection from a used toilet seat as the parts of your body which are vulnerable will not in fact touch the seat itself. It has been proven that there are more germs in a used kitchen dishcloth than on the average toilet seat.

People with reduced mobility such as the elderly, hospitalised patients, wheelchair users or those with neurological conditions may find using a toilet difficult. Keeping your privates dry is the most important prevention of infection. Anyone with a UTI need not feel the embarrassment that they may be thought of as unclean...we just handle the bacteria differently and have our own natural balance of 'good' bacteria. The less we interfere with our delicate areas, the more protected they will be.

A full bladder

We are taught in our early years about toilet hygiene, from childhood into adolescence and adulthood. It all makes perfect sense as we strive to be clean, but there are some no-no's in the personal washing department that must be avoided if you don't want a water infection.

Try not to hold onto a full bladder for any length of time. Your body tells you when you need a toilet and by waiting unnecessarily you risk having concentrated urine, containing E.coli bacteria from your gastrointestinal tract. By all means wipe a toilet seat in a public place if you want to, but try to avoid sitting on toilet paper as the paper can in fact harbour bacteria and can also absorb some urine and spread it. When passing urine try to be patient. Many of us lead busy lives and a trip to the toilet is usually an interruption to it - or more of an inconvenience than a convenience! Doing it properly is not a quick in/out visit for women and we can help to avoid water infections by making sure the bladder is <u>completely</u> empty.

Now then, whilst you sit contemplating whether or not to stand up once you think your bladder is empty, just relax and do nothing for a few seconds, then gently push with your lower abdomen muscles. You may be surprised to find a little extra urine being released that you weren't aware of. Try this more than once, even by sitting up straight, leaning to one side then the other until you are sure that your bladder is empty. (On a very personal note, I suggest when you empty your bowels, just put paper in the toilet bowl to avoid splashing your privates with dirty water). Never make more than one wipe with one handful of paper. It's important to wipe and throw away. The safest way is to 'swipe' away from the front, towards the back every time. If you only passed urine, the swipe isn't necessary. Just dab with some paper to absorb any urine, making sure not to touch any other parts. Never have the paper in contact with the urethra, just dry the surrounding skin and leave the urethra alone. Needlessly touching of moist sensitive areas will pass unwanted bacteria into your body.

Washing your privates

Knowing that water droplets will carry any bacteria much further than you think, I cannot recommend using a bidet for cleaning your privates after using the toilet. Women are very vulnerable to the transfer of bacteria in private areas, unlike men who can wash with a bidet and rarely get infected.

Under this section about keeping clean, is the one most effective prevention that has changed my life. I suddenly realised, like a light switching on, that my own washing routine was the probable cause of my regular infections. In my house we mostly use a shower cubicle, but this could apply to bathing as well. For me, this discovery is the main event, simply the most effective way of preventing infection that has changed my life so much. It's quite shocking that it has taken me over 40 years to get to this point, where I now feel that I am in control of my water infections, and have banished them to my past. Simply by accepting that an infection is the result of my own carelessness, and by taking alternate measures, I now no longer have regular infections. It can be as easy as changing the habits of a lifetime.

I used to think there was something wrong with me. I was suffering repeated water infections at least 6 times per year and it was starting to affect my kidneys. I was taking far too many antibiotics. However, during my work for an agency in a role as Health Services Assistant I realised just how many other women must have a similar problem. Ladies were asked to to undergo physical examinations before they could be accepted in a speciality role, but many of them sadly failed the examination due to having water infections, and they became upset as they seemed to have infections all of the time. Having discovered very easy steps to take, I have been infection free for almost 4 years now. This has made me want to share my ideas and experience with as many other women as possible and for us all to reduce the intake of antibiotics.

Firstly, it's very important that you ignore all sponges, bath gloves, facecloths and any other netting or fabric washing accessory in the bathing area. All of these items will carry new and old bacteria to your urethra. You will only need two hands, a bar of mild soap and to follow my instructions.

It is most important to remember that your dominant hand is only ever for washing your front parts, your other hand is only for your back parts. The vagina in the middle is the 'boundary' you can wash up to but must not cross.

Openings such as the urethra and the vagina are better for not coming into direct contact with soap. The natural Ph of the body can be unsettled if you end up over-washing your privates, and the vagina will keep itself clean on the inside.

Make your bare hands quite soapy (remembering non-perfumed soap, something you have become trusting of), and most importantly _put the bar of soap down_ before you begin.

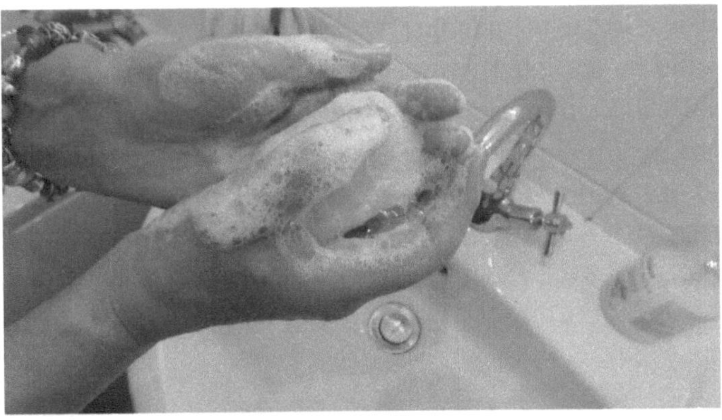

I'm right handed, so with my soapy right hand I cup my front parts between my legs and run my index and middle finger around the folds of skin, keeping to the front of my genitals. The length of your fingers is enough to clean over the top of the folds of skin. Never purposely open the labia to wash inside with soap, just wash the outsides and rinse the area well (dominant hand only) with clean warm water. With your soapy 'other' hand (not a bar of soap) reach around your thigh to your bottom - never reach down between the front of your legs as you risk spreading the soap too far and you also risk overbalancing! So, reaching around the back to your butt cheeks just use your fingers to gently explore the skin around your cheeks and your back passage, then rinse off both hands in running water if possible, literally washing your hands. Never cross contaminate the front or back with the wrong hand. Reach behind with your fingertips to rinse as water runs down your back (or kneeling/standing in the bath ready to sit). In case any of you were wondering, I doubt very much that bathwater is a regular cause of water infections and there is no evidence to suggest this, however by sharing a bath the increase in bacteria could potentially cause irritation. It is recommended to use a shower so that water is rinsed away, however you can purchase a hand held shower to fix to the bath taps. Remember what I said about not disturbing the flesh too much? Try to leave the insides of the labia alone, so you avoid exposing the urethra. The warm bath water will suffice for rinsing well when you sit down. Never pay too much attention to washing your body on the inside. Your body has a natural Ph level and by adding soap or other products you are interfering with nature. Don't add any scented products to your bath unless you know they won't irritate you afterwards.

The exception to my washing routine is when washing from a sink unit. Standing up by a sink means your flooring will inevitably get quite wet, so make sure you start off with adequate coverage with old towels or mats so that you don't slip. I too have used a sink to wash, and you still need to adhere to the dominant hand routine. Always wash and rinse the front before attempting to wash the back. To make sure all of the soap is removed, I suggest using a small clean facecloth for the front and once you have removed soap gently without disturbing the lips too much, swish the cloth well in water before you wipe the soap from the back. Never use a bidet, it will spread bacteria even if you think your back passage should be clean. The cloth must be well rinsed and avoid actually disturbing the lips to avoid direct contact with the urethra. Be sure to put the facecloth in with your dirty washing and use a clean one next time.

Keep a personal bath towel for just you to use. Dry the outsides of the front genitals with minimum effort trying not to disturb the flesh too much, and change for a clean towel every week. I recommend you do not share a house towel as I've seen many times before - partners and families sharing one large bath sheet, NO... only ever use a towel for just you and keep cross-infection at bay.

So, to summarise it's really quite simple:-

1. Most importantly of all please STOP, STOP, STOP using cloths or sponges or bathing gloves to wash your privates. I can say this will most certainly help you because the very day I stopped using a little yellow netting pom-pom thingy to wash between my legs with, was the day all of my infection stopped.

2. Your vagina has a well balanced Ph level (4.5). It has its own good bacteria and it is self-douching (self-cleansing). It should never need to have any kind of soap or product up there - ever, so

don't mess with the insides. Soaps have perfume and can be highly irritant. They will change the natural delicate Ph balance of your body and cause unnecessary irritation. Direct application of soap to the urethra will sting, and many of us will remember the sensation from childhood.

3. Let your own body deal with whatever might be inside at any time, it will naturally expel semen or menstrual fluids and will keep the insides clean with the help of gravity. Just gently wash the outside skin (the vulva) and take care when cleaning the anus or skin around it, not to spread soap.

4. When it comes to rinsing, a shower of water is preferable. Remember one hand for each side. You can cup one hand, strategically placed by your vulva until it contains water and splash the skin. However if bathing in deep water just let the water rinse off the soap from the rectum when it's submerged. Try not to rub or spread the soapy water.

5

SEXUALLY ACTIVE WOMEN

Sexually active women are at risk of regular water infections for all of the reasons mentioned above, with the addition of a third party who may not at first appreciate the precautions you need to take. You cannot pass a UTI onto a partner but sex at this time may be very uncomfortable. Good sex is not about making sure we have clean hands, it's impetuous and spontaneous. However, we must get our priorities in the right order to prevent any cross-contamination whilst still enjoying the moment.

Be sensible, and by that I mean be aware of what is being touched and by what. Fingers that caress buttocks and anywhere close to your rectum can be highly erotic, but I insist that you discourage those same fingers then caressing the skin at the front of your genitals. It's quite simply a case of one hand used for caressing the back areas and the other hand used for the front. Many women prefer to steer their partner clear of their anus. As long as moisture isn't running from one side to the other in the excitement, then any offensive bacteria should be kept at one end. Do I need to say more? Maybe I should explain further...

Sexual activity is a perfect scenario for the spread of unwanted bacteria. Whenever the area surrounding your anus is touched during sex, unwanted bacteria will be carried on your partner's skin, whether it's fingers or anything else, to the very next thing being touched. Basically, think of it like this....once you put a drop of bacteria into a cup of water, the whole cup becomes infected. Even if there is no direct contact with the labia or urethra, the immediate concern is the amount of surrounding moisture on the body (including sweat) which allows bacteria to get absolutely everywhere.

Because women are built with a vulnerable opening right next to a highly erotic area, bacterial transfer is inevitable. However, as mentioned earlier, not all women suffer with UTIs. My best friend is in her 70's and she had to ask me what a UTI was. She has never experienced one. Some fortunate women seem to have an inbuilt natural defence to them, possibly with higher levels of the right hormones and will therefore never suffer with one.

Sometimes you can't do right for doing wrong. Whatever you try to do will only make you stressed. Believe me, even the missionary position is just as potentially contaminating as the doggie position. The pressure of a partner's body during intercourse will force bodily fluid to spread on the skin and bacteria will enter the urethra. Your genitals naturally have their own perfectly good bacteria, which we need every day of our lives, but to introduce someone else's bacteria can be a problem if the right precautions are not followed. A warm, moist environment simply means that the transfer of unwanted bacteria is quick and unnoticeable, and even a brief encounter with skin-on-skin activity is just as risky as full blown intercourse. There is little we can do to avoid this spread, and let's face it, if there is a mistake it can easily be cured. Knowing whereabouts you are being touched is the key.

UTI in Pregnancy

For women like myself who suffer terrible morning sickness, dehydration is a big problem. During my first 5 months even water would not stay down and became a liquid projectile in less than a minute. The result was a kidney infection which made the skin over my whole body feel unbearable to touch. In order to overcome dehydration I had to suck on ice cubes with cordial in them. These were my only source of fluid intake for a few weeks.

UTIs are quite common during pregnancy, when the urine is more concentrated with hormones and types of sugar. This can encourage bacterial growth, making it harder for your body to defend against unwanted bacteria trying to get in. Pregnant women will experience ureteral dilation, which is when the urethra gradually expands until baby's delivery, making it easier for bacteria to invade. In addition the foetus puts pressure on the bladder as the baby grows and this can trap bacteria or cause urine to leak. You may recall I mentioned earlier to avoid holding on to a full bladder as the gastrointestinal bacteria E.coli will start to grow. In pregnancy this scenario is common with a dilated urethra, because with less tone in the muscles of the bladder and extra bladder volume, the urine is more prone to bacterial growth.

Estrogen and the menopause effect

Women can get a UTI at any age, but a peak time for UTIs in women is after the onset of the menopause. Estrogen is a natural hormone produced by women in the ovaries (but men do naturally produce a small amount). Estrogen starts to reduce in our bodies long before the menopause begins. This is known as the peri-menopausal stage. As estrogen is the hormone which drives the menstrual cycle, a lack of it creates irregular or missed periods. Eventually periods stop altogether (which has to be a good thing) but there is a negative side to take into our middle age.

A lack of estrogen at any stage can for instance change the way women store fat, which is naturally on hips and thighs. The drop in this hormone promotes fat storage around the abdomen, but a balanced diet and plenty of exercise should help to keep this under control. During the menopause the lack of estrogen can change our lives in many ways. Low estrogen levels are responsible for many changes to our bodies:

1. It causes thinning of the lining of the urethra which makes it more vulnerable to infection.
2. It creates regular hot flushes where it suddenly seems like you're inside a hot oven. During the night these wake you as your body sweats to try and cool down.
3. A lack of estrogen can even cause a feeling of depression. Estrogen is thought to boost the level of serotonin - a chemical in the brain which increases mood, and therefore a lack of it creates mood swings and sometimes depression. This can be treated by your GP.

Low estrogen levels can be as a result of other factors besides the menopause, such as ovarian failure, a family history of hormone deficiencies, excessive exercising, thyroid problems, being severely underweight, pituitary gland problems or chemotherapy treatment.

Estrogen is absolutely essential for bone health. Post-menopausal women are at an increased risk of osteoporosis with bone density loss and subsequent bone fractures. Without taking additional hormone replacement therapy

(HRT), the levels of vaginal estrogen are much lower and again this allows bacteria to flourish more easily. (I choose not to take HRT for personal reasons, knowing where it comes from and how female horses (mares) are unfairly treated in order to obtain it).

According to online sources, a report in a medical journal suggests research carried out back in 2013 revealed that estrogen delivered vaginally for postmenopausal women has reduced the onset of urinary tract infections.

There are products on the market that provide extra moisture to the vagina, however from past experience not all of the products are suitable for everyone. Fortunately, the dryness we experience in delicate areas immediately before intercourse, can be remedied without buying creams or gels. I quickly resolved this issue with a natural, simple solution by transferring plenty of my own saliva from my finger tips onto the areas of delicate skin before penetration. It's been a perfectly natural solution for me without risking further potential irritation from gels and creams.

Spermicide

It's widely known that bacterial infections can happen following the use of spermicide products.

Spermicide is a type of contraceptive that can be put onto condoms or used inside the vagina as gel, foam, cream or suppositories. It kills sperm or stops it from moving. However, spermicide may increase the risk of urinary tract infections. Vaginal irritation such as burning or itching or a rash is the most common side effect of spermicide. Spermicide may also cause an allergic reaction. Spermicide may cause penile irritation or burning urination in your sexual partner and it does not prevent sexually transmitted diseases. Still 28% of women will get pregnant when using it. Just don't unless you really must.

Facts about chemotherapy

After receiving chemotherapy treatment, it is not uncommon to contract a bacterial infection. A side effect from chemotherapy is that it can dry out the vaginal tissue making sex uncomfortable. Some drugs used in chemotherapy break down into substances which irritate the bladder and the urethra. After chemotherapy, your white blood cell count can be reduced, which will make you more vulnerable any infections which can also worsen quite quickly. Because of the chemotherapy your immune system isn't as well-equipped to deal with an invasion of bacteria, and therefore simple infections can become life-threatening within hours if not treated by a GP.

To pee or not to pee...

In our youth sex is much more experimental and most are only concerned about what sex feels like, not the consequences. I'm not trying to preach to anyone, but if a little thought goes into hygiene then it can save a lot of pain with UTIs afterwards. The solution I have is not something new, it's quite simple....to pee!

Having been made aware that the moisture created by our bodies is a transport system for bacteria, the most important thing to remember is to nip into the bathroom to pass urine the minute sex is over. Don't wait, don't lie back and relax, time is of the essence here. There's no need to dive off the bed, but be mindful that your next duty is to flush out those bad boys. Just get to your feet and use the toilet. This is very important to flush out potential infection travelling to your bladder. Bacteria from another person's skin, whether it be from their fingers, their genitals, their mouths, will have started a journey into your urethra once love making begins. It's inevitable. So, in order to avoid a UTI, make sure you have a good drink (water if possible) prior to initiating sex, which will then work by expelling any unwanted bacteria from your urethra when you pee after sex, as soon as you can get to a toilet.

Always pee immediately after sexual activity.

Doctors have said that the best way to avoid any infection is to pee before <u>and</u> after sex. Yes in some ways I agree. If you don't pee first and have a slight accident during the excitement, it will be embarrassing and an invitation for bacteria directly to your bladder. So, for peace of mind, by all means before you get naked, visit the bathroom leaving yourself feeling comfortable. Just don't hang around and empty every little bit. Do try to be prepared and make sure before you begin anything romantic, that you have a good swig of water or else you will have nothing left to pee with afterwards!

For most of us there is a probability that in haste to have pleasure, your partner's penis or even a sex toy may fall out of the vagina and slip down towards your rectum. Then STOP! Please do not just carry on as before - you need to stop and wash before unwanted harmful bacteria is then carried in your moisture into the urethra and your vagina. You will get an infection if you choose to carry on and the pain really isn't worth it. On the subject of sex toys, even the substance used to make the toys can make you itchy and sore. Irritation can be caused by products on your partners hands or face. To help the avoidance of irritation make sure you wash any toys and your sensitive areas afterwards. Also follow the tips as above and pee plenty in order to help to expel any stray bacteria.

Oral contraception:

There is currently no known direct connection between taking oral contraception and developing a UTI. There is however, a substantiative connection between a greater number of people having more sex (because they feel safer taking oral contraception) relative to a higher percentage of secondary causes for UTI I've already discussed. In other words, more people are comfortable having more protected sex, which in turn increases the chance of bacterial invasion.

6

STAYING HEALTHY - AN OVERVIEW FOR HEALTHY LIVING

<u>Thrush:</u>

Thousands of women also suffer another horrible condition we know as 'thrush'. This is normally a yeast infection in the mouth and can be caused by an immune disorder, but it happens to healthy people as well. Thrush is normally treated with topical over-the-counter medications quite easily. Similar yeast infections can occur in the vagina, also known as thrush, and this is treated with creams or pessaries from the pharmacy. Occasionally the yeast infection can reach the bladder in the same ways I mentioned earlier, causing cystitis.

There may be a relationship between the vaginal thrush and a urinary tract infection in two ways. Firstly it is possible that the yeast caused the urine infection. The second possibility is that medications or other treatments (such as douching) that are used for treatment of the thrush, have caused an imbalance in the normal bacteria we need in the vagina to stay healthy, therefore causing a urine infection. Thrush in the vagina can cause intense itching or soreness.

The best way to avoid thrush developing is to keep your private parts clean, dry and as natural as possible. Avoid wearing man-made fibres in the underwear you choose, as some materials can cause increased sweating (such as nylon tights) providing a haven for yeast infections. It is also known that tight fitting clothes and intrusive tight underwear such as thongs can prevent any air getting to these areas and make you more vulnerable to infections.

As with all infections, a proper diagnosis will be made on examination by your GP and you should follow professional advice accordingly.

Checking the colour:

Remember, healthy urine is a quite clear, pale straw-coloured fluid. It's quite important to check that your urine in the toilet bowl is not very yellow. If your urine is a mid-yellow colour or darker then your body is already dehydrated. Don't think of the colour in the toilet basin as a true reading...you have pee'd into a bowl of water so the colour you see is actually diluted. It needs to be almost clear to be healthy. You may find yourself feeling sluggish or more fatigued with headaches or even dizziness if your urine is dark yellow. Some medications are known to change the colour of your urine, so check with your doctor if you take such medication, in case the colour is to be expected. If urine becomes cloudy, and has an odour which can be like a yeast smell or even something like the smell of sugar puffs, then you probably have an infection. Once it arrives you need medical treatment fast, so seek advice from a doctor or GP. A urine sample into a sterile pot will reveal which bacteria needs to be treated and can also reveal any other issues such as an excess of protein, or the presence of more than normal leukocytes (white blood cells, which suggest an infection) or perhaps any traces of blood which can affect the colour of your urine.

Dark, foul-smelling urine is often
an indication of a UTI

For those women having periods, the chance of seeing the true colour of urine is slight. Whilst on a period you could use unperfumed feminine wipes to stay clean, but try not to disturb the flesh too much. Best if possible to stay away from products that leave moisture on warm skin, as bacteria will thrive in it. Don't buy perfumed wipes or perfumed body sprays to apply directly to this area of your body, as these may cause irritation such as soreness or itching. Just bathe or shower every day.

I feel it is important to recognise is that regular hydration of the body is essential. The adult human body is made up of 50 to 65% water which is naturally expelled in our breath, sweat, tears, saliva and urine. Natural functions of our organs during the digestive process will produce toxins that need to be expelled. Try to monitor how much fluid you drink in one day in order to keep a healthy balance in your gut. Keeping hydrated will also help to keep your skin looking younger. I'm not a lover of water on it's own, but I do drink more of it when I add a splash of fruit juice, pieces of fruit or even weak cordial in it. I cannot however recommended alcohol for hydration. Tea and coffee are acceptable if reduced to just one or two per day but caffeine is not terribly good for hydration purposes and not helpful for ageing joints either - but that's another subject you can read about online.

Getting the right underwear:

If you are fashion conscious like myself, you may have tried wearing a thong (or G-string) to avoid VPL (visible panty lines). Thongs have been blamed for ulcerations on the skin and chaffing, causing soreness of the most sensitive areas of skin. They also increase the risk of vaginal or urethra infections due to the proximity of the thong to bacterial zones where they touch the rectum, making it easier for bacteria to travel. Thongs have been blamed for causing vaginal discharge in some women, who then use panty liners for protection, and by doing so they inadvertently create a moisture haven for bacteria.

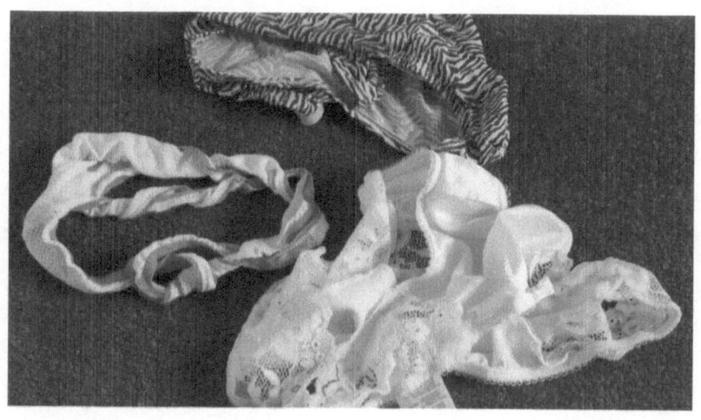

Man-made fabric in today's fashion is not ideal for close fitting underwear. The fabric is usually stretchy and made for comfort and style rather than for the benefit of our health. Such fabric is used for tights and is more likely to trap moisture in these areas. The use of cotton underwear will certainly help to keep your delicate skin drier and less likely to sweat. Cotton fabric is more breathable for skin which promotes drier skin with less risk of bacterial infection. Always try to wear clean underwear. Never be tempted to re-use panties that were worn the night before as stale underwear is just asking for trouble.

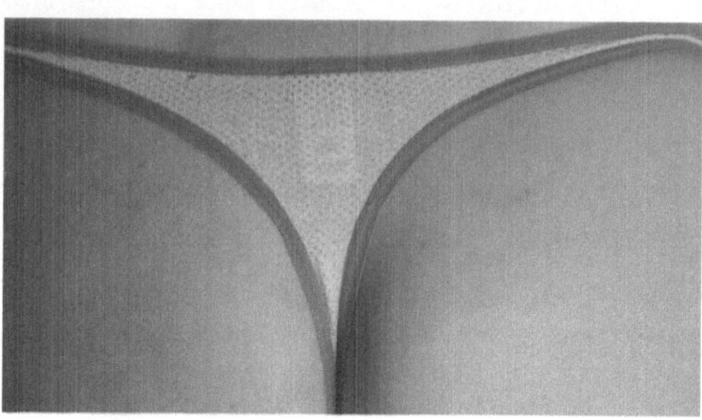

Food Additives:

In this section, I want to add snippets of information I feel we all have the right to know. These facts may not be related to UTIs but they are very important to know if we want to stay healthy as we move into middle age and older. I believe we should all spend a few moments learning more about potential effects of some common food additives that could affect your digestion if taken in large amounts.

In today's world of convenience foods, we have all been tempted by the look of a tasty ready-made meal and a flavoured drink. Our busy lives just don't give us enough time to prepare fresh food anymore. Currently there seems to be a complete trust in the ingredients used in fast food, and a distinct lack of awareness of the potential effects that food additives can have on our bodies. Information can be found online to learn about the long term side-effects popular artificial sweeteners such as aspartame, acelsulfame K, and sucralose. These are really not good at all for our general health and it is widely known that they can be carcinogenic if taken over a long period of time in large volumes. So now when I shop, I find myself checking labels and containers to make sure that I am not ingesting these chemicals on a daily basis. Please take a moment to read about them online and then decide for yourself if you, like me, would prefer to avoid the potential health risks.

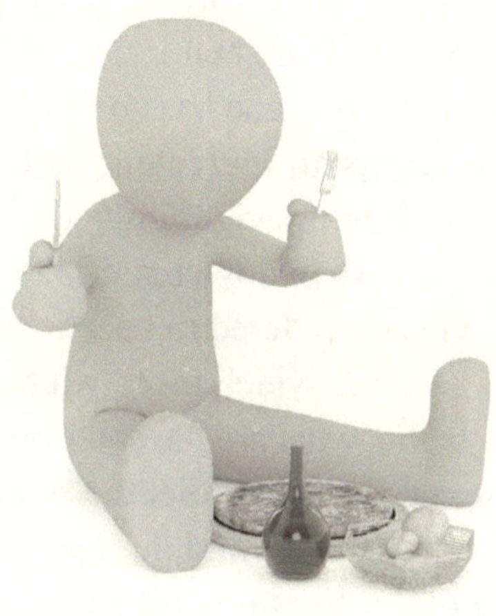

Speaking of staying healthy, I found that there are some everyday items of food and drink we need to re-evaluate in our daily lives. For example, in light of recent events in my life I have changed from skimmed milk which has high calcium value, to semi-skimmed milk. The reason may seem quite bizarre, however after losing my gall bladder to calcification in the summer of 2012 I decided to re-address my calcium intake. I remember my late mother took matters into her own hands when she developed osteoarthritis, and started adding more calcium to her diet. Unfortunately, in her haste she took too much and damaged her liver as a consequence. Calcium is essential for good health - but was I unknowingly taking too much? Once the fat is removed from full fat milk there is more calcium by volume in the skimmed milk than semi-skimmed. I asked my GP for a blood test but my calcium was not too high. I had studied the changes I made to my diet in recent years and skimmed milk was the only difference. Following this I began reading about the make-up of skimmed milk and it shocked me to discover something called titanium dioxide. This chemical whitener is used to make foods more appealing and has no food value as such. You will see it listed as an ingredient on tubes of white toothpaste. It's in white bread, skimmed milk (which is naturally bluish grey when any cream is removed)....and white PAINT, and is considered to be safe to consume in small amounts. Yes, this widely used whitener is part of our everyday lives, but what are the consequences? I have chosen to take great care of my diet these days and to try and stay healthy as I reach middle-age. Additives will always be a part of our lives now as we are generally too busy to make and grow our own food under tight scrutiny. Please just take a while to research these things, so that you too can stay healthy.

<u>Summary of Quick Reminders:</u>

Without bacteria life would not exist, so we must respect where it lives and prevent it spreading in order to keep cross-contamination to a minimum.

Learn how to look after your bladder.

Keep exercising that sphincter muscle, it will pay dividends for your bladder as you get older (and better control has pleasurable benefits in the intercourse department too when used to squeeze!).

It's most important after sexual activity to have some urine in your bladder, to flush bacteria out into the toilet after sex.

Please don't worry or stress yourself about making sex too clinical. Try to take the time to share your best plan with your partner especially if you feel vulnerable, (in advance of any sexual activity) so that you can both relax and enjoy the moment. Any loving partner will understand.

Always seek medical advice once an infection has taken hold.

Always check with your doctor before you change or add medications.

Only bathe genitals using soapy hands, one hand for the front, the other hand for the back. (Use of only one hand means washing the hand and the soap before changing sides).

Don't put off a full bladder until it becomes urgent, as stale urine increases the risk of infection.

Always wipe from front to back.

Try to avoid underwear made from man-made materials that could make you sweat.

Check the ingredients of fast food and drink products to avoid chemicals which may cause irritation.

So now you're as well-informed as me and between us we can fight the UTI with women power. Surprisingly, with just a few simple changes to your daily routine you can make a world of difference.

I just wish someone had told me all those years ago!

ABOUT THE AUTHOR

Beverly Rose was born in 1961 in Cheshire, England, as the third child to a working class family. An intelligent and inquisitive child who was unfortunate to suffer cystitis frequently and developed many UTIs throughout adulthood. She worked hard at school and started work in an office on the day she left at the age of 16. She had a glowing career in communications lasting 28 years. A personal injury at work to her hearing meant that the job she loved came to an abrupt end in 2006. Following some treatments and several other jobs, she is now happy working as a secretary at the NHS.

Beverly has been happily married to Sci-Fi author Christopher Thompson for over 15 years and has one daughter and two step-daughters. Beverly's motto in life has always been 'Be Prepared' and this is her first book in which she aims to project this strategy for other women to follow.